SOUTHWESTERN COOKING

Designed by Sally Strugnell
Recipe photography by Peter Barry
Recipes styled by Bridgeen Deery and Wendy Devenish
Edited by Jillian Stewart

CLB 2811
© 1992 Colour Library Books Ltd, Godalming, Surrey, England.
All rights reserved.
This 1992 edition published by Crescent Books,
distributed by Outlet Book Company Inc., a Random House Company,
40 Engelhard Avenue, Avenel, New Jersey 07001.
Printed and bound in Singapore.
ISBN 0 517 06605 X
8 7 6 5 4 3 2 1

SOUTHWESTERN COOKING

CRESCENT BOOKS
NEW YORK • AVENEL, NEW JERSEY

INTRODUCTION

The Southwestern region of America is a vast area, with a landscape and climate that varies from cool mountain ranges to hot, dry deserts and sun-drenched Gulf beaches. It is hardly surprising then that this part of the U.S. has such a varied cuisine. The traditional ingredients of Southwestern cooking – chilies, corn, squash, avocados, beans and beef – reoccur in many dishes, but in a great variety of combinations. Texans in particular will argue endlessly with other Texans that their particular barbeque recipes are the most authentic, even though traditional recipes vary widely according to which part of the State they come from!

The roots of Southwestern cooking lie in the food cultivated by the Native Americans. Maize was made into tortillas and breads that sustained them throughout the year. They also cultivated many of the ingredients that would later form part of the popular Tex-Mex cuisine – beans, corn, and squash. The Native American and Hispanic influence is still very recognizable in Tex-Mex cooking today. Tortillas, either cornmeal or flour, are still important as a base for toppings and sauces, or a substitute for bread and rolls. Salsas, refried beans and chili, that well-known beef stew, are all part of both Southwestern and Mexican cooking.

The present-day status of beef in Southwestern cooking was secured by the early cattle-men. In the East the demand for beef was huge, but it was the cowboys who adopted the ever-popular barbeque, as their nomadic lifestyle demanded a portable, easy method of cooking. The cowboys were sustained in their long journeys by a staple diet of beef, beans and endless amounts of thick black coffee. And this hearty ranch fare is still very much in evidence today, although it is much more varied and interesting than it was when the cowboys were fed from a chuckwagon in the 19th century!

As well as a plentiful supply of beef, the Southwest also boasts a rich natural bounty in its rivers and coastal waters. Trout and catfish from the rivers and an abundance of red snapper, mackerel, shrimp and oyster from the ocean find their way both onto the barbeque and into the most sophisticated restaurant.

Right: the church of San Geronimo at the Taos pueblo was built to replace the original church destroyed in 1847.

Tortillas

Preparation Time: about 50 minutes **Cooking Time:** 3 minutes per tortilla
Makes: 10

Borrowed from Mexico, these have become indispensable in Tex-Mex cooking and are used in a variety of delicious ways.

Ingredients

2 cups all-purpose flour
  (more if necessary)
2 tsps baking powder
Pinch salt

4 tbsps vegetable shortening
½-¾ cup hot water
Oil for frying

Sift the flour, baking powder and salt into a bowl. Rub in the vegetable shortening until the mixture resembles coarse crumbs. Add water, mixing until absorbed. Knead gently and add more flour if the dough is too sticky. Cover and leave to rest for 15 minutes.

    Divide the dough into ten even-sized pieces. Roll into balls on a floured surface, cover and leave to stand for 20 minutes. Roll out each ball on a lightly floured surface to a circle 7 inches in diameter. Cover the finished tortillas while rolling all the remaining dough. Place a lightly oiled frying pan over high heat. Fry the tortillas individually on both sides until bubbles form on the surface. Stack them as they are cooked and set them aside until ready to use.

Cattle ranching is still a major economic and social force in the Southwest.

Red Pepper Preserves

Preparation Time: about 30 minutes **Makes:** 2 cups

This sweet but hot and spicy condiment adds a bright spot of color and Tex-Mex flavor to a main course or appetizer.

Ingredients
5 red peppers, seeded
3 red or green chilies, seeded
1½ cups sugar

¾ cup red wine vinegar
1 cup liquid pectin

Chop the peppers and chilies finely in a food processor. Combine the sugar and vinegar in a deep, heavy-based pan and heat gently to dissolve the sugar. Add the peppers and chilies and bring the mixture to the boil. Simmer for about 15 or 20 minutes. Stir in the pectin and return the mixture to the boil over high heat. Pour into sterilized jars and seal.

Keep for up to one year in a cool, dark place.

The Big Bend River provides good fishing as it meanders through the national park on its way to Lake Amistad.

Cornmeal Pancakes

Preparation Time: 30 minutes **Cooking Time:** 3-4 minutes per pancake
Serves: 4

Cornmeal, either yellow, white or blue, is an important ingredient in Tex-Mex recipes. Here it's combined with corn in a light and different kind of appetizer.

Ingredients
1 cup yellow cornmeal
1 tbsp flour
1 tsp baking soda
1 tsp salt
2 eggs, separated
2 cups buttermilk

Oil
10oz frozen corn
Sour cream
Red pepper preserves
Green onions, chopped

Sift the dry ingredients into a bowl, adding any coarse meal that remains in the strainer. Mix the egg yolks and buttermilk together and gradually beat into the dry ingredients. Cover and leave to stand for at least 15 minutes.

Whisk the egg whites until stiff but not dry and fold into the cornmeal mixture. Lightly grease a frying pan with oil and drop in about 2 tbsps of batter. Sprinkle with the corn and allow to cook until the underside is golden brown. Turn the pancakes and cook the second side until golden. Continue with the remaining batter and corn. Keep the cooked pancakes warm.

To serve, place three pancakes on warm side plates. Add a spoonful of sour cream and red pepper preserves to each and sprinkle over finely sliced or shredded green onions.

Top: comancheros entertain the tourists outside the restaurants and bars in Gaslight Square, Corpus Christi.

Hot Pepper Relish

Preparation Time: about 30 minutes **Cooking Time:** about 45 minutes
Makes: 4 cups

Prepare this colorful relish in the summer, when peppers are plentiful, but save some to brighten up winter meals, too.

Ingredients

3lbs sweet peppers (even numbers of red, green, yellow and orange, or as available), seeded
4-6 red or green chilies, seeded and finely chopped
2 medium onions, finely chopped
2 cups granulated or preserving sugar

1½ cups white wine vinegar or white distilled vinegar
½ tsp oregano
½ tsp ground coriander
2 bay leaves
Salt to taste

Cut the peppers into small dice and combine with the chilies and onions in a large saucepan. Pour over boiling water to cover, and return to the boil. Cook rapidly for 10 minutes and drain well.

Meanwhile, combine the sugar and vinegar in a large saucepan. Bring slowly to the boil to dissove the sugar, stirring occasionally.

When the pepper and onions have drained, add them and the remaining ingredients to the vinegar and sugar. Bring back to the boil and then simmer for 30 minutes. Remove the bay leaves and pour into sterilized jars and seal.

Tiwa-speaking Native Americans still live in Pueblo de Taos, the tallest pueblo in the Southwest.

Denver Omelet

Preparation Time: 25 minutes **Cooking Time:** 10-15 minutes **Serves:** 2

This is a quick and easy meal for busy people. If prepared like scrambled eggs, the mixture can double as a sandwich filling.

Ingredients

4 strips bacon, diced
Half a small onion, chopped
Half a small green pepper, seeded
  and chopped
1 tomato, seeded and diced

3 eggs, beaten
Salt and pepper
1 tbsp grated cheese
Dash Tabasco (optional)
Chopped parsley to garnish

Heat a medium-size frying pan or omelet pan. Add the bacon and sauté slowly until the fat is rendered. Turn up the heat and cook until the bacon begins to brown and crisp. Add the onion and green pepper and cook to soften and finish off the bacon.

Mix the tomato with the eggs, salt, pepper, cheese and Tabasco, if using. Pour into the pan and stir once or twice with a fork to mix all the ingredients. Cook until lightly browned on the underside. Place under a pre-heated broiler and cook the top quickly until brown and slightly puffy. Sprinkle with parsley, cut into wedges and serve immediately.

The contrasting architecture of Main Street and Third in Fort Worth perfectly illustrates the growth of big business in the area.

Chicken Nueva Mexicana

Ingredients
6 chicken thighs, skinned and boned
2 tbsps mild chili powder
2 tbsps oil
Juice of 1 lime
Pinch salt
Corn Crepes
1 cup fine yellow cornmeal
½ cup flour
Pinch salt
1 whole egg and 1 egg yolk
1 tbsp oil or melted butter or margarine
1½ cups milk
Avocado and Orange Salad
2 oranges
1 avocado, peeled and sliced
Juice of 1 lime

Lime Cream Sauce
¾ cup sour cream or natural yogurt
1 tsp lime juice and grated rind
6 tbsps heavy cream
Salt
Garden Salsa
1 large zucchini
1 large ripe tomato
2 shallots
1 tbsp chopped fresh coriander
Pinch cayenne, pepper and salt
1 tbsp white wine vinegar
3 tbsps oil

Pinch sugar
Pinch coriander
6 tbsps pine nuts, toasted

Place the chicken in a shallow dish. Combine the chili powder, oil, lime juice and salt and pour over the chicken. Turn the pieces over and rub the marinade into all the surfaces. Cover and refrigerate for 2 hours. Combine all the ingredients for the Lime Cream Sauce and fold together gently. Cover and leave 2 hours in the refrigerator to thicken. Sift the cornmeal, flour and salt for the crepes into a bowl. Combine the eggs, oil and milk. Make a well in the center of the dry ingredients, pour in the liquid and stir gradually to form a batter. Leave the batter to stand for 30 minutes. Trim the ends of the zucchini and cut into small dice. Peel the tomato, remove the seeds and cut into small dice. Cut the shallots into small dice. Combine the coriander, cayenne pepper, vinegar, oil and salt, mixing very well. Pour over the vegetables and stir to mix. Cover and leave to marinate.

Heat a small amount of oil in a large frying pan and place in the chicken in a single layer. Fry quickly to brown both sides. Pour over remaining marinade, cover and cook until tender, about 25 minutes. Heat a small amount of oil in a frying pan. Wipe out excess oil with a paper towel and return the pan to the heat until hot. Pour a spoonful of the batter into the pan and swirl to coat the bottom with the mixture. Make sure the edge of each crepe is irregular. When the edges of each crepe look pale brown and the top surface begins to bubble, turn the crepes using a palette knife. Cook the other side. Stack as each is finished, cover with foil and keep warm in a low oven. Pour about 2 tbsps oil into a small frying pan and when hot add the pine nuts. Cook over moderate heat, stirring constantly until golden brown. Remove and drain on paper towels. Peel and segment the oranges over a bowl to catch the juice. Cut the avocado in half, remove the stone and peel. Cut into thin slices and combine with the orange. Add the lime juice, sugar and coriander, and toss gently to mix.

To assemble, place one corn crepe on a plate. Place one piece of chicken on the lower half of the crepe, top with a spoonful of Lime Cream Sauce. Place a serving of Garden Salsa and one of Avocado and Orange Salad on either side of the chicken and partially fold the crepe over the top. Scatter over pine nuts and serve immediately. **Serves 6**

Southwestern Stir-Fry

Preparation Time: 25 minutes plus 4 hours marinating
Cooking Time: about 20 minutes **Serves:** 4

East meets West in a dish that is lightning-fast to cook. Baby corn, traditionally Oriental, echoes the Southwestern love of corn.

Ingredients

1lb sirloin or rump steak
2 cloves garlic, crushed
6 tbsps wine vinegar
6 tbsps oil
Pinch sugar, salt and pepper
1 bay leaf
1 tbsp ground cumin
1 small red pepper, seeded
    and sliced
1 small green pepper, seeded
    and sliced
2oz baby corn
4 green onions, shredded
Oil for frying

Red Sauce
8 fresh ripe tomatoes, peeled,
    seeded and chopped
4 tbsps oil
1 medium onion, finely chopped
1-2 green chilies, finely chopped
1-2 cloves garlic, crushed
6 sprigs fresh coriander
3 tbsps tomato paste

Slice the meat finely across the grain. Combine in a plastic bag with the next 6 ingredients. Tie the bag and toss the ingredients inside to coat. Place in a bowl and leave about 4 hours.

Heat the oil for the sauce and cook the onion, chilies and garlic to soften but not brown. Add remaining sauce ingredients and cook about 15 minutes over gentle heat. Purée in a food processor until smooth. Heat a frying pan and add the meat in three batches, discarding the marinade. Cook to brown and set aside. Add about 2 tbsps of oil and cook the peppers about 2 minutes. Add the corn and onions and return the meat to the pan. Cook a further minute and add the sauce. Cook to heat through and serve immediately.

Chicken with Red Peppers

Preparation Time: 35-40 minutes **Cooking Time:** about 30 minutes **Serves:** 4

Easy as this recipe is, it looks and tastes good enough for guests. The warm taste of roasted red peppers is typically Tex-Mex.

Ingredients

4 large red peppers
4 skinned and boned chicken breasts
1½ tbsps oil
Salt and pepper

1 clove garlic, finely chopped
3 tbsps white wine vinegar
2 green onions, finely chopped
Sage leaves for garnish

Cut the peppers in half and remove the stems, cores and seeds. Flatten the peppers with the palm of your hand and brush the skin sides lightly with oil. Place the peppers skin side up on the rack of a pre-heated broiler and cook about 2 inches away from the heat source until the skins are well blistered and charred. Wrap the peppers in a clean towel and allow them to stand until cool. Peel off the skins with a small vegetable knife. Cut into thin strips and set aside.

Place the chicken breasts between two sheets of plastic wrap and flatten by hitting with a rolling pin or meat mallet. Heat 1½ tbsps oil in a large frying pan. Season the chicken breasts on both sides and place in the hot oil. Cook 5 minutes, turn over and cook until tender and lightly browned. Remove the chicken and keep it warm. Add the pepper strips, garlic, vinegar and green onions to the pan and cook briefly until the vinegar loses its strong aroma. Slice the chicken breasts across the grain into ¼ inch thick slices and arrange on serving plates. Spoon over the pan juices. Arrange the pepper mixture with the chicken and garnish with sage leaves.

Chili Roja

Preparation Time: 25 minutes **Cooking Time:** 1½-2 hours **Serves:** 6-8

Red meat, red onions, red peppers, paprika, tomatoes and red beans all give clues to the name of this zesty stew.

Ingredients

2lbs beef chuck, cut into 1 inch pieces
Oil
1 large red onion, coarsely chopped
2 cloves garlic, crushed
2 red peppers, seeded and cut into 1 inch pieces
1-2 red chilies, seeded and finely chopped
3 tbsps mild chili powder
1 tbsp cumin
1 tbsp paprika
3 cups beer, water or stock
8oz canned tomatoes, puréed
2 tbsps tomato paste
8oz canned red kidney beans, drained
Pinch salt
6 ripe tomatoes, peeled, seeded and diced

Pour about 4 tbsps oil into a large saucepan or flameproof casserole. When hot, brown the meat in small batches over moderately high heat for about 5 minutes per batch. Set aside the meat on a plate or in the lid of the casserole. Lower the heat and cook the onion, garlic, red peppers and chilies for about 5 minutes. Add the chili powder, cumin and paprika and cook for 1 minute further. Pour on the liquid and add the canned tomatoes, tomato paste and the meat. Cook slowly for about 1½-2 hours. Add the beans about 45 minutes before the end of cooking time. When the meat is completely tender, add salt to taste and serve garnished with the diced tomatoes.

Top: Fort Union National Monument in New Mexico. The fort was established in 1851 to protect the Santa Fe Trail.

Barbecued Ribs

Preparation Time: 30 minutes **Cooking Time:** 1 hour 15 minutes **Serves:** 6

No Tex-Mex cookbook would be complete without a barbecue recipe. This versatile sauce keeps well in the refrigerator, too.

Ingredients

4½ lbs pork spare ribs
1 cup tomato ketchup
2 tsps mustard powder
4 tbsps Worcester sauce
2 tbsps vinegar

4 tbsps brown sugar
Half a chili, seeded and finely chopped
Half a small onion, finely chopped
4 tbsps water
Salt (if necessary)

Place the ribs in a roasting pan and cover with foil. Cook for 15 minutes at 425°F.

Meanwhile, combine all the remaining ingredients in a heavy-based pan and bring to the boil. Reduce heat and simmer for about 15 minutes. Reduce the oven temperature to 350°F and uncover the ribs. Pour over the sauce and bake a further hour, basting frequently. Remove the ribs from the roasting pan and reserve the sauce. Place the ribs on a cutting board and slice into individual rib pieces, between the bones. Skim any fat from the surface of the sauce and serve the sauce separately.

The simplicity of early ranch life is exemplified in the dining room of the Box and Strip House in the Ranching Heritage Center in Lubbock.

Broiled Trout with Pepper Relish

Preparation Time: about 20 minutes **Cooking Time:** 4-5 minutes **Serves:** 4

Fresh trout, perfectly broiled, and spicy sweet pepper relish make an unusual, innovative and very special dish.

Ingredients
1 lime
2 tbsps butter, melted
4 filleted trout, unskinned (double fillets preferred)

8 tbsps hot pepper relish (see recipe on page 16)
Lime wedges or coriander leaves to garnish

Remove the rind of the lime with a citrus zester and set it aside. Squeeze the juice and mix with the butter. Place the fish fillets on a broiler rack and baste with the butter and lime juice mixture. Place under a pre-heated broiler for about 4-5 minutes, depending on the thickness of the fillets. Baste frequently. Pour over any remaining butter and lime juice and sprinkle the fish with the lime zest. Gently re-heat the relish and spoon 2 tbsps down the center of each of the double fillets. Garnish with lime or coriander.

The now peaceful Big Bend National Park was once part of an area inhabited by the fierce Mescalero Apache.

Barbecued Pork Stew

Preparation Time: 25 minutes **Cooking Time:** about 1½ hours **Serves:** 4

Named for the sauce rather than the cooking method, this stew requires long, slow cooking to bring out its flavor.

Ingredients

2lb pork shoulder, cut in 2-inch cubes
Oil
2 medium onions, cut in 2-inch pieces
1 large green pepper, seeded and
    cut in 2-inch pieces
1 tbsp chili powder
2 cloves garlic, crushed
1lb canned tomatoes

3 tbsps tomato paste
1 tbsp Worcester sauce
½ cup water or beef stock
2 tbsps cider vinegar
1 bay leaf
½ tsp dried oregano
Salt and a few drops Tabasco sauce

Heat about 2 tbsps oil in a large sauté or frying pan. When hot, add the pork cubes in two batches. Brown over high heat for about 5 minutes per batch. Remove to a plate. Add more oil if necessary and cook the onions and peppers to soften slightly. Add the chili powder and garlic and cook 1 minute more. Add the tomatoes, their juice and the tomato paste. Stir in the Worcester sauce, water or stock and vinegar, breaking up the tomatoes slightly. Add bay leaf, oregano and salt. Transfer to a flameproof casserole dish. Bring the mixture to the boil and then cook slowly for about 1½ hours, covered.

When the meat is completely tender, skim any fat from the surface of the sauce, remove the bay leaf and add a few drops of Tabasco sauce to taste. Adjust salt and serve.

Top: the staple diet of ranch hands has changed surprisingly little – beans are still one of the easiest ways to sustain a man through a hard day's work.

Riverside Trout

Preparation Time: 25 minutes **Cooking Time:** 15-20 minutes **Serves:** 4

Brook trout is so delicious that simple preparation is all that's necessary. Crisp cornmeal, bacon and pine nuts complement the fresh flavor.

Ingredients

⅓-½ cup vegetable oil
4 tbsps pine nuts
8 strips bacon, diced
1 cup yellow cornmeal
Pinch salt and white pepper

4 trout weighing about 8oz
  each, cleaned
Juice of 1 lime
Fresh sage or coriander

Heat 6 tbsps of oil in a large frying pan. Add the pine nuts and cook over moderate heat, stirring constantly. When a pale golden brown, remove them with a draining spoon to paper towels. Add the diced bacon to the oil and cook until crisp, stirring constantly. Drain with the pine nuts.

Mix the cornmeal, salt and pepper, and dredge the fish well, patting on the cornmeal. Shake off any excess. If necessary, add more oil to the pan – it should come about halfway up the sides of the fish. Re-heat over moderately high heat. When hot, add the fish two at a time and fry until golden brown, about 4-5 minutes. Turn over and reduce the heat slightly if necessary and cook a further 4-5 minutes. Drain and repeat with remaining fish. Drain almost all the oil from the pan and re-heat the bacon and nuts very briefly. Add the lime juice and cook a few seconds. Spoon the bacon and pine nut mixture over the fish and garnish with sage or coriander.

The blazing sun creates an orange landscape in White Sands National Monument, New Mexico.

Chili Verde

Preparation Time: 30-40 minutes **Cooking Time:** 1-1½ hours **Serves:** 6-8

A chili, really a spicy meat stew, is as traditional in the Southwest as it is in Mexico.

Ingredients

2lbs lean pork, cut into 1-inch pieces
Oil
3 green peppers, seeded and cut into 1-inch pieces
1-2 green chili peppers, seeded and finely chopped
1 small bunch green onions, chopped
2 cloves garlic, crushed
2 tsps ground cumin
2 tsps chopped fresh oregano

3 tbsps chopped fresh coriander
1 bay leaf
3 cups beer, water or chicken stock
8oz canned chickpeas, drained
1½ tbsps cornstarch mixed with 3 tbsps cold water (optional)
Salt
1 large ripe avocado, peeled and diced
1 tbsp lime juice

Heat 4 tbsps of oil and lightly brown the pork cubes over high heat. Use a large flameproof casserole and brown the pork in 2 or 3 batches. Lower the heat and cook the peppers to soften slightly. Add the chilies, onions, garlic and cumin and cook for 2 minutes. Add the herbs and liquid and reduce the heat. Simmer, covered, 1-1½ hours or until the meat is tender. Add the chickpeas during the last 45 minutes. If necessary, thicken with the cornstarch, stirring constantly after adding until the liquid thickens and clears. Add salt to taste and remove the bay leaf. Toss the avocado in lime juice and sprinkle over the top of the chili to serve.

Richly-colored cliffs overlook Lighthouse Peak Trail in Palo Duro Canyon, Texas.

Gulf Coast Tacos

Preparation Time: about 1 hour   **Serves:** 6

Around the gulf of Mexico, ever popular tacos take on a new look and taste with a seafood filling.

Ingredients
6 tortillas (see recipe on page 10)

Green Chili Salsa
1 tbsp oil
3 tomatillos, husks removed
1 clove garlic
1oz coriander
2 green chilies
Juice of 1 lime
½ cup sour cream
Pinch salt and sugar

Filling
8oz large raw shrimp, peeled
8oz raw scallops, quartered if large
1 tsp coriander seed, crushed
1 shallot, finely chopped
Salt and pepper
6 tbsps white wine
Water
1 small jicama, peeled and cut
    into matchstick strips
Coriander leaves and lime wedges
    to garnish

Prepare the tortillas according to the recipe.

Heat 1 tbsp oil in a small frying pan and slice the tomatillos. Sauté them for about 3 minutes to soften. Place in a food processor along with the garlic, coriander, chilies and lime juice. Purée until smooth. Fold in the sour cream, adjust seasoning and chill.

Heat oil in a deep sauté pan to a depth of at least 2 inches. When hot, place in a tortilla and press down under the oil with a metal spoon. When the tortilla starts to puff up, take it out and immediately fold to form a shell. Hold in shape until it cools slightly and sets. Repeat with the remaining tortillas. Keep them warm in an oven, standing on their open ends.

Place the shrimp, scallops, coriander seeds, shallot and salt and pepper in a sauté pan with the wine and water to barely cover. Cook for about 8 minutes, stirring occasionally. The shrimp should turn pink and the scallops will look opaque when cooked. Fill the taco shells with the jicama. Remove the seafood from the liquid with a draining spoon and arrange on top of the jicama. Top with the salsa and decorate with coriander leaves. Serve with lime wedges.

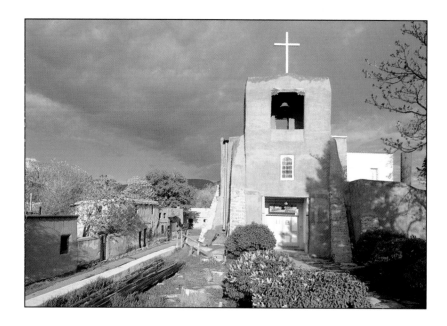

Fried Bass with Cornmeal

Preparation Time: 20 minutes **Cooking Time:** 5 minutes per batch **Serves:** 4

As a coating for frying, cornmeal is superb. It fries to a crisp crunch and adds a subtle flavor of its own.

Ingredients

2 cups yellow cornmeal
2 tbsps flour
Pinch salt
2 tsps cayenne pepper
1 tsp ground cumin
2 tsps garlic powder

2lb freshwater bass or other white
    fish fillets
Milk
Oil for frying
Lime wedges to garnish

Mix the cornmeal, flour, salt, cayenne, cumin and garlic together in a shallow container or on a piece of wax paper. Skin the fillets if desired. Dip them into the milk and then lift to allow the excess to drip off. Place the fish in the cornmeal mixture and turn with two forks or, if using paper, lift the ends and toss the fish to coat.

Meanwhile, heat oil in a deep frying pan, large saucepan or deep fat fryer. Add the fish in small batches and cook until the fillets float to the surface. Turn over and cook to brown lightly and evenly. Drain on paper towels and serve immediately with lime wedges.

Top: storm clouds gather over the Mission of San Miguel in Santa Fe.

Cheese or Vegetable Enchiladas

Preparation Time: 1 hour **Cooking Time:** 10-15 minutes **Serves:** 4

Many dishes in Southwestern cooking have Mexican origins, like these filled tortillas.

Ingredients
8 tortillas (see recipe on page 10)
Full quantity Red Sauce (see recipe
   on page 22)

Cheese Filling
2 tbsps oil
1 small red pepper, seeded and
   finely diced
1 clove garlic, crushed
1 tbsp chopped fresh coriander
½ cup heavy cream
½ cup cream cheese
½ cup mild cheese, grated
Whole coriander leaves

Vegetable Filling
2 tbsps oil
1 small onion, finely chopped
1 green pepper, seeded and diced
2 zucchini, diced
½ tsp oregano
½ tsp ground cumin
4oz corn, fresh or frozen
Salt and pepper
1½ cups grated mild cheese
Sour cream
Full quantity green chili salsa
   (see recipe on page 38)

Prepare the tortillas, red sauce and green chili salsa according to the recipe directions.

Heat the oil for the cheese filling and cook the pepper and garlic slowly to soften. Add the coriander and pour in the cream. Bring to the boil and cook rapidly to thicken. Add the cream cheese and stir to melt. Add the grated mild cheese, stir in and keep the filling warm. Re-heat the tortillas wrapped in foil in a moderate oven for about 10 minutes. Place one at a time on serving dishes and spoon in the cheese filling. Fold over both sides to the middle. Re-heat the red sauce, if necessary, and spoon over the center of two enchiladas. Garnish with coriander leaves.

For the vegetable filling, heat the oil and cook the onion to soften. Add the remaining vegetables except the corn. Add the oregano and cumin and cook about 3 minutes or until the onions are soft. Add the corn and heat through, adding seasoning to taste. Stir in the grated cheese and fill the tortillas as before, but place in a baking dish. Cook covered, for about 10-15 minutes at 350°F, or until the cheese has melted and the filling is beginning to bubble.

Serve topped with sour cream and green chili salsa.

Chalupas

Preparation Time: about 40 minutes **Cooking Time:** about 20 minutes **Makes:** 10

These are tortillas in another form, this time a snack with spicy meat. Create your own combination with a selection of different toppings.

Ingredients
Half quantity tortilla recipe
12oz ground beef
Full quantity Red Sauce (see recipe on page 22)
Oil for frying
2 cloves garlic, crushed
1 tsp dried oregano
2 tsps cumin
Salt and pepper
3oz frozen corn
4 tbsps raisins

Toppings
6-8 chopped green onions
4-6 diced tomatoes
Half a small head lettuce, shredded
½ cup sour cream
1 cup shredded cheese

Prepare the tortillas according to the recipe and divide the dough in 10. After the required resting time, roll the balls of dough into 3½-inch rounds. Prepare the Red Sauce according to the recipe instructions and set it aside. Heat at least 2 inches of oil in a frying pan, sauté pan or medium saucepan. When hot, place in one tortilla and fry briefly until just crisp. Drain and keep them warm.

Cook the beef slowly until the fat begins to render. Add the garlic, oregano and cumin and raise the heat to brown the meat. Season to taste and then stir in enough of the Red Sauce to moisten the meat well. Add the corn and raisins, cover the pan and leave to stand for 5 minutes. Spoon the meat onto the tortillas and drizzle over more sauce. Garnish with your choice of toppings.

Preparing a meal for a hoard of hungry cattlemen is no easy task in the blazing Texas heat.

Swordfish with Grapefruit Tequila Salsa

Preparation Time: 35 minutes **Cooking Time:** 4-6 minutes **Serves:** 4

Rich and dense in texture, swordfish takes very well to a tart grapefruit accompaniment with a dash of tequila.

Ingredients

4-6 ruby or pink grapefruit
    (depending on size)
1 lime
Half a green chili, seeded and
    finely diced
1 green onion, finely chopped
2 tbsps chopped fresh coriander
1 tbsp sugar

3 tbsps tequila
4-8 swordfish steaks (depending
    on size)
Juice of 1 lime
2 tbsps oil
Black pepper to taste
Coriander sprigs for garnish

Remove the zest from the grapefruit and lime with a zester and set it aside. Remove all the pith from the grapefruit and segment them. Squeeze the lime for juice. Mix the grapefruit and citrus zests with the chili, onion, coriander, sugar, tequila and lime juice and set aside. Mix the remaining lime juice, oil and pepper together and brush both sides of the fish. Place under a pre-heated broiler and cook for about 4 minutes each side depending on distance from the heat source.

To serve, place a coriander sprig on each fish steak and serve with the grapefruit salsa.

The Pecos National Monument contains some fascinating pueblo ruins and the ruin of the old Pecos Mission.

Indian Bread with Chorizo and Salsa

Preparation Time: 45 minutes-1 hour   **Cooking Time:** 25-30 minutes
Serves: 4-6

A version of this bread recipe was once baked by Native Americans.

Ingredients

Bread
2 cups all-purpose flour
1 tbsp baking powder
Pinch salt
1 tbsp vegetable shortening
2 tsps cumin seed
¾ cup plus 2 tbsps water

Chorizo Topping
1lb chorizo sausage
2 medium red potatoes, scrubbed
4 green onions, chopped

Salsa
1 clove garlic
1oz coriander leaves
1 tsp fresh oregano
Half fresh red or green chili, seeded
Pinch salt and dry mustard
Juice of 2 limes
¾ cup oil
Shredded lettuce, crumbled goat's
 milk cheese and chopped tomatoes
 to garnish

Sift the flour, baking powder and salt into a bowl. Rub in the shortening until the mixture resembles coarse crumbs and then stir in the cumin seed. Stir in enough water to make a soft, slightly sticky dough. Knead several times, cover and leave to stand for 15-20 minutes. Divide the dough into 8 pieces and roll into 5 inch circles on a well-floured surface. Make a hole in the center of each with your finger and leave the circles to stand, covered, for 30 minutes.

Meanwhile, boil the potatoes in their skins. Place the chorizo in a sauté pan and cover with water. Cover the pan and bring to the boil. Lower the heat and simmer about 10 minutes, or until just tender. Remove the chorizo from the water and peel off the casings while the sausage is still warm. Chop sausage roughly and set aside. When the potatoes are tender, drain them and leave to cool. Cut the potatoes into ½-inch dice. Place the garlic, coriander, oregano, chili, salt and mustard into a food processor and add the lime juice. Process until well blended. With the machine running, pour the oil through the funnel in a thin, steady stream. Process until smooth and adjust the seasoning. Pour the oil for cooking the bread into a large saucepan to a depth of about 2-3 inches. Heat to 375°F. Carefully lower in one dough circle and push it underneath the oil with a large metal spoon. Fry for about 30 seconds, turn over and fry the other side. Drain each while frying the others.

Mix the chorizo, green onions and potatoes with enough of the salsa to moisten. Arrange the shredded lettuce on top of the bread and spoon on the chorizo topping. Spoon on any remaining salsa, sprinkle with chopped tomato and crumbled cheese.

Churros

Preparation Time: 25-30 minutes   **Cooking Time:** 6 minutes per piece
Makes: 12-14

These fritters can be either sweet or savory. Either way, they're a treat with a Mexican influence.

Ingredients
Basic Dough
Scant 1 cup plus 2 tbsps water
3 tbsps butter or margarine
Pinch salt
1 cup all-purpose flour
6 tbsps cornmeal
2 eggs
Oil for deep frying

Savory ingredients
2 tbsps finely grated cheese
2 chili peppers, seeded and finely
  chopped
Parmesan cheese (optional)

Sweet ingredients
4 tbsps sugar
1 tbsp unsweetened cocoa powder
1 tsp ground cinnamon
Powdered sugar (optional)

Combine the water, butter or margarine and salt in a heavy-based saucepan. If making sweet churros, add sugar as well. Cook over medium heat until the butter or margarine melts. Immediately stir in the flour and cornmeal. Keeping the pan over medium heat, stir until the mixture pulls away from the sides of the pan and forms a ball. Take off the heat and cool slightly. Add the eggs one at a time, beating vigorously in between each addition. It may not be necessary to add all the egg. Beat until the mixture is smooth and shiny and thick enough to pipe. Add the cheese and chilies or the cocoa and cinnamon with the eggs. Spoon the mixture into a pastry bag fitted with a star tip.

   Heat the oil in a deep saucepan or sauté pan to a depth of at least 4 inches. Pipe the dough into the oil in 10 inch strips and fry until golden brown, about 3 minutes per side. Drain on paper towels and sprinkle the savory churros with Parmesan cheese and the sweet with powdered sugar, if desired. Serve warm.

Spicy Rice and Beans

Preparation Time: 25 minutes **Cooking Time:** 50 minutes **Serves:** 6-8

A lively side dish or vegetarian main course, this recipe readily takes to creative variations and even makes a good cold salad.

Ingredients

4 tbsps oil	Salt
2 cups long grain rice	3½ cups stock
1 onion, finely chopped	1lb canned red kidney beans,
1 green pepper, seeded and chopped	drained and rinsed
1 tsp each ground cumin and	1lb canned tomatoes, drained and
coriander	coarsely chopped
1-2 tsps Tabasco	Chopped parsley

Heat the oil in a casserole or a large, deep saucepan. Add the rice and cook until just turning opaque. Add the onion, pepper and cumin and coriander. Cook gently for a further 2 minutes. Add the Tabasco, salt, stock and beans and bring to the boil. Cover and cook about 45 minutes, or until rice is tender and most of the liquid is absorbed. Remove from the heat and add the tomatoes, stirring them in gently. Leave to stand, covered, for 5 minutes. Fluff up the mixture with a fork and sprinkle with parsley to serve.

Top: the view north from Sotol Vista Overlook across the mountains of Big Bend National Park in Texas.

Refried Beans

Preparation Time: overnight soaking and 2 hours cooking for the beans
Serves: 6-8

This is a classic accompaniment to both Mexican and Southwestern dishes be they poultry or meat, vegetable or cheese.

Ingredients

8oz dried pinto beans	Salt and pepper
Water to cover	Grated mild cheese
1 bay leaf	Shredded lettuce
6 tbsps oil	Tortillas

Soak the beans overnight. Change the water, add the bay leaf and bring to the boil. Cover and simmer about 2 hours, or until the beans are completely tender. Alternatively, bring the beans to the boil in cold water and then allow to boil rapidly for 10 minutes. Cover and leave to stand for one hour. Change the water and then continue with the recipe.

Drain the beans and reserve a small amount of the cooking liquid. Discard bay leaf. Heat the oil in a heavy frying pan. Add the beans and, as they fry, mash them with the back of a spoon. Do not over-mash – about one third of the beans should stay whole. Season to taste. Smooth out the beans in the pan and cook until the bottom is set but not browned. Turn the beans over and cook the other side. Top with the cheese and cook the beans until the cheese melts.

Serve with finely shredded lettuce and tortillas, either warm or cut into triangles and deep-fried until crisp.

The Texas Longhorn has found a permanent home in the Lyndon B. Johnson State Historical Park, which is dedicated to the early settlers to the area.

Chili Rellenos

Preparation Time: 40 minutes   **Cooking Time:** about 30 minutes in total
Serves: 8

Organization is the key to preparing these stuffed peppers. Fried inside their golden batter coating, they're puffy and light.

Ingredients

Full quantity Red Sauce (see recipe on page 22)
8 small green peppers
4 small green chilies, seeded and finely chopped
1 clove garlic, crushed
1 tsp chopped fresh sage
8oz cream cheese
2 cups grated mild cheese
Salt
Flour for dredging
Oil for deep frying
8 eggs, separated
6 tbsps all-purpose flour
Pinch salt
Finely chopped green onions

Blanch the whole peppers in boiling water for about 10-15 minutes, or until just tender. Rinse them in cold water and pat them dry. Carefully cut around the stems to make a top, remove and set aside. Scoop out the seeds and cores, leaving the peppers whole. Leave upside down on paper towels to drain. Mix together the chilies, garlic, sage, cheeses and salt to taste. Fill the peppers using a teaspoon and replace the tops, sticking them into the filling. Dredge the peppers with flour and heat the oil in a deep fat fryer to 375°F.

Beat the egg yolks and flour in a mixing bowl until the mixture forms a ribbon trail when the beater is lifted. Beat the whites with a pinch of salt until stiff but not dry. Fold into the egg yolk mixture. Shape 2 tbsps batter into an oval and drop into the oil. Immediately slide a metal draining spoon under the batter to hold it in place. Place on a filled pepper. Cover the tops of the peppers with more batter and then spoon over hot oil to seal. Fry until the batter is brown on all sides, turning the peppers over carefully. Drain on paper towels and keep them warm on a rack in a moderate oven while frying the remaining peppers. Sprinkle with onions and serve with Red Sauce.

Salad Huevos Rancheros

Preparation Time: 45 minutes **Cooking Time:** about 15 minutes **Serves:** 4

Chicory is justifiably becoming more and more popular. This recipe puts it to delicious use with eggs and other Tex-Mex favorites – peppers, zucchini, jicama and chorizo.

Ingredients

1 large red pepper, roasted (see recipe on page 24)

1 chorizo sausage, blanched and cut into thin strips

4 heads chicory

1 large or 2 small zucchini, cut into matchstick pieces

1 small jicama root, cut into matchstick pieces

2-3 green onions, shredded

4 tbsps pine nuts

4 eggs

Dressing

1 tsp chopped fresh coriander

6 tbsps oil

2 tbsps lime juice

Dash Tabasco

Salt and pinch sugar

Prepare the roasted pepper and cut it into thin strips. Blanch the chorizo as for Indian Bread Chorizo and Salsa. Separate the leaves of the chicory and slice or leave whole if small. Bring water to the boil and blanch the zucchini and jicama strips for one minute. Rinse under cold water until completely cool and leave to drain. Combine with the chicory and green onions. Add the strips of chorizo and set aside.

Toast the pine nuts in a moderate oven until golden brown, about 5 minutes. Bring at least 2 inches of water to the boil in a frying or sauté pan. Turn down the heat to simmering. Break an egg onto a saucer or into a cup. Stir the water to make a whirlpool and then carefully pour the egg into the center, keeping the saucer or cup close to the level of the water. When the water stops swirling and the white begins to set, gently move the egg over to the side and repeat with each remaining egg. Cook the eggs until the whites are completely set, but the yolks are still soft. Remove the eggs from the water with a draining spoon and place them immediately into a bowl of cold water.

Mix the dressing ingredients together and pour half over the vegetables and sausage. Toss to coat. Arrange the mixture on individual plates in the shape of nests. Remove the eggs from the cold water with the draining spoon and hold them over a towel for a few minutes to drain completely. Place one egg in the middle of each nest. Spoon the remaining dressing over each egg, sprinkle over the pine nuts and garnish the yolk with a coriander leaf.

Black Bottom Ice Cream Pie

Preparation Time: 25 minutes plus several hours to freeze **Makes:** 1 pie

Unbelievably simple, yet incredibly delicious and impressive, this pie is the perfect ending to a summer meal.

Ingredients

8-10 graham crackers
½ cup butter or margarine, melted
4oz shredded coconut

2oz semi-sweet chocolate, melted
3 cups coffee ice cream
Dark rum

Crush crackers with a rolling pin or in a food processor. Mix with melted butter or margarine. Press into an 8½ inch false bottomed flan dish. Chill thoroughly in the refrigerator.

Meanwhile, combine 4 tbsps coconut with the melted chocolate. When cooled but not solidified, add about a quarter of the coffee ice cream, mixing well. Spread the mixture on the base of the crust and freeze until firm. Soften the remaining ice cream with an electric mixer or food processor and spread over the chocolate-coconut layer. Re-freeze until firm. Toast the remaining coconut in a moderate oven, stirring frequently until pale golden brown. Allow to cool completely. Remove the pie from the freezer and leave in the refrigerator for 30 minutes before serving.

Push up the base of the dish and place the pie on a serving plate. Sprinkle the top with toasted coconut. Cut into wedges and drizzle with rum before serving.

The ghost town of Mogollon in New Mexico is one of the state's most evocative old mining towns.

Frozen Lime and Blueberry Cream

Preparation Time: 40 minutes plus overnight freezing **Serves:** 6

Blueberries grow wild in this part of the United States and recipes including them abound.

Ingredients

Juice and rind of 4 limes	4oz blueberries
Water	3 egg whites
1 cup sugar	1 cup heavy cream, whipped

Measure the lime juice and make up to 6 tbsps with water if necessary. Combine with the sugar in a heavy-based pan and bring to the boil slowly to dissolve the sugar. When the mixture forms a clear syrup, boil rapidly to 250°F on a sugar thermometer.

Meanwhile, combine the blueberries with about 4 tbsps water in a small saucepan. Bring to the boil and then simmer, covered until very soft. Purée, sieve to remove the seeds and skin, and set aside to cool. Whisk the egg whites until stiff but not dry and then pour on the hot sugar syrup in a steady stream, whisking constantly. Add the lime rind and allow the meringue to cool. When cold, fold in the whipped cream. Pour in the purée and marble through the mixture with a rubber spatula. Do not over-fold. Pour the mixture into a lightly-oiled mold or bowl and freeze until firm, preferably overnight. Leave 30 minutes in the refrigerator before serving or dip the mold for about 10 seconds in hot water. Place a plate over the bottom of the mold, invert and shake to turn out. Garnish with extra whipped cream, blueberries or lime slices.

Dallas' futuristic office blocks form a strange backdrop to the "pioneer village" in Old City Park.

Guava Mint Sorbet

Preparation Time: 2-3 hours **Makes:** 3 cups

When a light dessert is called for, a sorbet can't be surpassed. The exotic taste of guava works well with mint.

Ingredients
⅔ cup granulated sugar
1 cup water
4 ripe guavas
2 tbsps chopped fresh mint

1 lime
1 egg white
Fresh mint leaves for garnish

Combine the sugar and water in a heavy-based saucepan and bring slowly to the boil to dissolve the sugar. When the mixture is a clear syrup, boil rapidly for 30 seconds. Allow to cool to room temperature and then chill in the refrigerator.

Cut the guavas in half and scoop out the pulp. Discard the peels and seeds and puree the fruit until smooth in a food processor. Add the mint and combine with cold syrup. Add lime juice until the right balance of sweetness is reached. Pour the mixture into a shallow container and freeze until slushy. Process again to break up ice crystals and then freeze until firm. Whip the egg white until stiff but not dry. Process the sorbet again and when smooth, add the egg white. Mix once or twice and then freeze again until firm. Remove from the freezer 15 minutes before serving and keep in the refrigerator. Scoop out and garnish each serving with mint leaves.

Top: as well as more traditional methods of transport, Texan farmers require airplanes to manage the vast areas many of the ranches cover.

Fruit Empanadas

Preparation Time: 40 minutes-1 hour for the tortillas and 20 minutes for the rest of the dish **Makes:** 10

Tortillas can have a sweet side too, when stuffed with cheese and sunny apricots or exotic tropical fruit.

Ingredients
Full quantity Tortilla recipe
10 ripe fresh apricots, halved and
  pitted, or 1lb canned apricots,
  well drained

1lb cream cheese
Oil for deep-frying
Powdered sugar

Prepare the tortilla dough, roll out but do not pre-cook.

Heat oil in a deep saucepan to a depth of at least 2 inches. Oil should reach a temperature of 375°F. Cut the apricots into quarters and the cheese into 10 even pieces. Place one piece of cheese and an even amount of apricots on the lower half of each tortilla. Fold over the upper half and seal the edges. Crimp tightly into a decorative pattern. Fry one empanada at a time until golden on both sides. Baste the upper side frequently with oil to make the tortillas puffy. Drain well on paper towels and serve warm, sprinkled with powdered sugar.

The paths and pools of Thanks-Giving Square in Dallas form a peaceful oasis in the center of the city.

Chocolate Cinnamon Monkey Bread

Preparation Time: 2 hours **Cooking Time:** 45-50 minutes **Makes:** 1 loaf

Pull this bread apart to serve in individual pieces rather than slicing it. Savory versions substitute Parmesan and herbs for sugar and spice.

Ingredients

Dough
4 tbsps warm water
1 tbsp sugar
1 envelope dry yeast
3-3¾ cups bread flour
6 tbsps sugar
Pinch salt
5 tbsps butter, softened
5 eggs

Topping
½ cup butter, melted
1 cup sugar
2 tsps cinnamon
2 tsps cocoa
6 tbsps finely chopped pecans

Sprinkle 1 tbsp sugar and the yeast on top of the water and leave it in a warm place until foaming. Sift 3 cups of flour into a bowl and add the sugar and salt. Rub in the butter until completely blended. Add 2 eggs and the yeast mixture, mixing in well. Add the remaining eggs one at a time until the mixture forms a soft spongy dough. Add remaining flour as necessary. Knead for 10 minutes on a lightly floured surface until smooth and elastic. Place the dough in a greased bowl and turn over to grease all the surfaces. Cover with plastic wrap and put in a warm place. Leave to stand for 1-1½ hours or until doubled in bulk. Butter a ring mold liberally. Knock the dough down and knead it again for about 5 minutes. Shape into balls about 2 inches in diameter.

Mix the topping ingredients together except for the melted butter. Roll the dough balls in the butter and then in the sugar mixture. Place a layer of dough balls in the bottom of the mold and continue until all the dough and topping has been used. Cover and allow to rise again about 15 minutes. Bake in a pre-heated 350°F oven for about 45-50 minutes. Loosen from the pan and turn out while still warm.

Barbecued Pork Stew 32
Barbecued Ribs 28
Black Bottom Ice Cream Pie 60
Broiled Trout with Pepper Relish 30
Chalupas 44
Cheese or Vegetable Enchiladas 42
Chicken Nueva Mexicana 20
Chicken with Red Peppers 24
Chili Rellenos 56
Chili Roja 26
Chili Verde 36
Chocolate Cinnamon Monkey Bread 68
Churros 50
Cornmeal Pancakes 14
Denver Omelet 18
Desserts:
    Black Bottom Ice Cream Pie 60
    Chocolate Cinnamon Monkey
      Bread 68
    Frozen Lime and Blueberry Cream 62
    Fruit Empanadas 66
    Guava Mint Sorbet 64
Fish and Seafood:
    Broiled Trout with Pepper Relish 30
    Fried Bass with Cornmeal 40
    Riverside Trout 34
    Swordfish with Grapefruit Tequila
      Salsa 46
Fried Bass with Cornmeal 40
Frozen Lime and Blueberry
  Cream 62
Fruit Empanadas 66
Guava Mint Sorbet 64
Gulf Coast Tacos 38
Hot Pepper Relish 16

Indian Bread with Chorizo and Salsa 48
Meat:
    Barbecued Pork Stew 32
    Barbecued Ribs 28
    Chili Roja 26
    Chili Verde 36
    Southwestern Stir-fry 22
Poultry:
    Chicken Nueva Mexicana 20
    Chicken with Red Peppers 24
Red Pepper Preserves 12
Refried Beans 54
Riverside Trout 34
Salad Huevos Rancheros 58
Side Dishes:
    Churros 50
    Gulf Coast Tacos 38
    Hot Pepper Relish 16
    Red Pepper Preserves 12
    Tortillas 10
Southwestern Stir-Fry 22
Snacks:
    Chalupas 44
    Cheese or Vegetable Enchiladas 42
    Chili Rellenos 56
    Cornmeal Pancakes 14
    Denver Omelet 18
    Indian Bread with Chorizo and
      Salsa 48
    Refried Beans 54
    Salad Huevos Rancheros 58
    Spicy Rice and Beans 52
Spicy rice and Beans 52
Swordfish with Grapefruit Tequila Salsa 46
Tortillas 10